Muslin

a stitched exploration of loose weave fabrics
by
Fibrefusion

Susan Cranwell
Sandra Duff
Marian Harrington
Birgitte Hendricks
Annette Herrington
Irene Jackson
Jan Lovell
Joan Maynard
Janet Nowell
Madelaine Nightingale
Helen Noble
Bonny Osborne
Pauline Verrinder

This book has been brought together with the collective concept and collaboration of all the members of Pauline Verrinder's Contemporary Textile Art Group, Fibrefusion who are based in Cambridge, England

Introduction

What is it about textile enthusiasts that drives us to the nearest fabric supplier to buy yet more fabric to add to our stash. Our cupboards and shelves are already over-burdened with that 'must have fabric' that we just couldn't resist buying. We admire it - caress it – stroke it - and so often, once purchased, we just can't bring ourselves to cut into it.

When the Fibrefusion girls, were discussing subject ideas for the next book, their focus soon settled on the usual seductive subject of fabric. They were quickly aware that one of the most useful and versatile fabrics was Muslin. Simultaneously, open weave fabrics and Scrim were also high on the list.

They were also well aware, that in the present tough economic times, Muslin was also a very cheap, value for money fabric, perfectly suited to a wide variety of approaches and technique. 'The decision was made – Muslin would be theme for the next book'.

As with all the Fibrefusion books, this publication is a 'workshop in a book', written to help everyone who enjoys working with textiles to extend and develop their creative spirit. This is a hands-on-book to encourage the stimulation of new ideas and ways of thinking with Muslin as a catalyst.

Plastic tubing bound with strips of Muslin. Flowers frayed Muslin and felt.

Kebab sticks bound with Muslin and thread. Held together with twisted strips of Muslin.

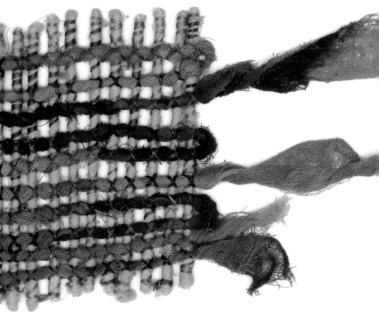

Fibrefusion would like to thank:

Tony Hatt – HATT OWEN DESIGN for his technical skills and patience
Shirley Makin for her imaginative and amusing cartoons
Kevin Mead – ART VAN GO for his skilled and creative photography.
Viv Arthur and Kevin Mead at ART VAN GO for their support and friendship
Our families for their long suffering patience and support.

Contents

Shirley

Why Muslin

As embroiderers' we love stitching and experimenting with a diverse collection of fabrics, fibres and threads. Muslin and similar open weave fabrics can be dyed, printed, discharged, distressed, manipulated, patched and pieced, stitched, constructed, and embellished. Strips of fabric can also be used as a thread.

The origin of the word Muslin is derived from French Mousseline or Italian Mussolina from Mussolo a city in Iraq. Muslin is woven from either cotton, linen or silk or a mixture of cotton and silk. There are also particular qualities of weave from fine, course and loose weave. It can be purchased in white, and cream or in a wide variety of commercial colours. Identifying Muslin or similar open weave fabrics can be problematic as they vary enormously from Butter Muslin,

Loomstate Muslin, Draping Muslin, Turban Muslin, Cheese Cloth, Cotton Muslin, Silk Cotton Muslin, Corinthia (bleached and starched). There is Cotton Gauze, Cotton Mousseline, and Novelle Linen.

Scrim is as popular with stitchers as Muslin ensuring a high profile in this book. Equally, the varied availability of Scrim surprises us, with examples accessible from fine cotton Scrim, hessian Scrim, linen Scrim, bandage Scrim or even builders Scrim.

You say 'Cailco' we say 'Muslin

Just to cause even more confusion, we realize that in some Countries, the fabric we call 'Muslin' is called 'Calico'. To avoid any controversy, in this book we are referring to FINE, LOOSELY WOVEN, OPEN WEAVE FABRIC. See the following images to remove any doubt.

Muslin embellished with stitch.

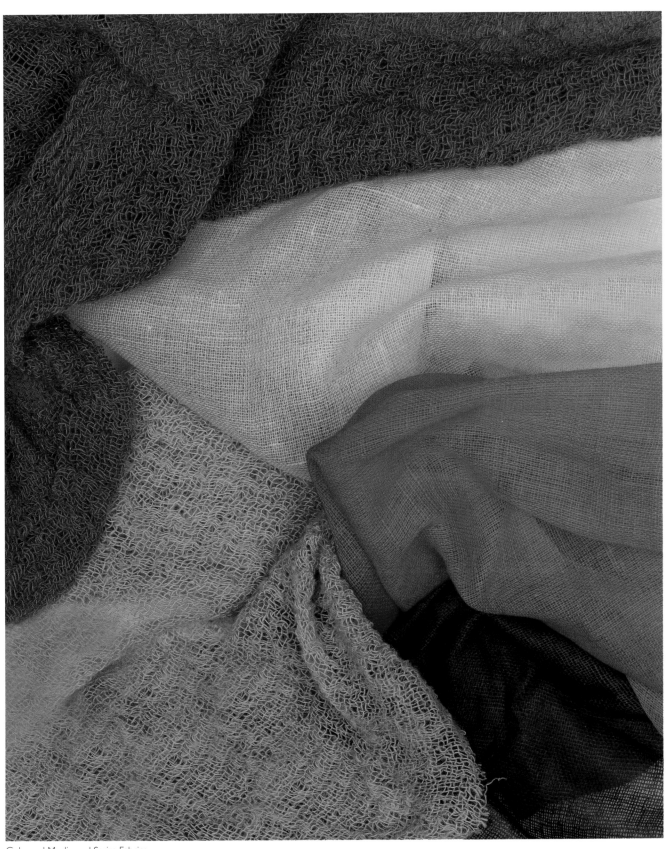

Coloured Muslin and Scrim Fabrics.
Some hand dyed.

Muslin to dye and print

Muslin can be purchased in a wide variety of colours from shops, markets and on line. However, dyeing your own fabric gives you more choice and control over the colour or colours you want to achieve. Essentially it also ensures that your work becomes unique and individual to you.

On the following pages we have detailed three diverse dyeing methods which have been pared down to the basics for easy use. All use Procion MX Dyes★ that are readily available from many art/textile suppliers.

Once you have dyed your fabric, open your eyes to the possibilities of additional surface decoration to your fabric. Printing designs onto your fabric is a popular option. Ready-made printing or stamping blocks are easily obtained, but we give ideas how to make your own printing blocks from readily available materials.

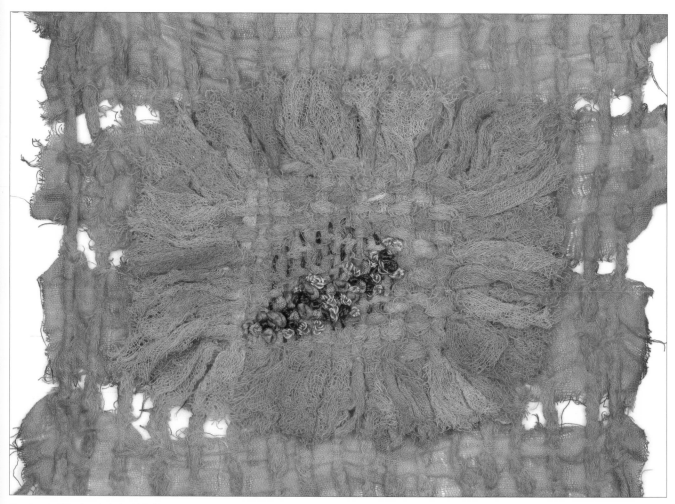

Dyed, embellished and stitched Muslin.

Why don't you try...
to dye your fabric using simple dyeing methods

Safety precautions for all dyeing methods
- Wear protective clothing, rubber gloves, goggles and a mask.
- Cover working surface
- Keep dyes out of reach of children
- Keep dyes out of contact with eyes and avoid inhaling.
- Ensure that the room is well ventilated.

Procon MX Dyes*
Procion MX Dyes are cold water fibre reactive dyes used for dyeing natural plant fibres, ie. cotton, linen, rayon, bamboo and viscose. These dyes are permanent, colourfast and washable. Dyeing methods detailed below use Procion MX Dyes. These dyes are suitable for dyeing Muslin, Scrim and natural fibre, open weave fabrics.

WASHING MACHINE DYEING
(Using Procion MX Dyes*)
- Pre-wash fabric as detailed above. Remove fabric – put in plastic bag until ready to dye – keep fabric damp.
- Place dye powder and salt in the machine drum. Ensure distribution of dye/salt through holes to avoid contact with the fabric.
- Place fabric in machine – still damp and unfolded.
- Set machine cycle 60°C/140°F (warm) – run for 20 mins. Pour diluted Soda Ash* into the detergent dispenser.
- Run until programme has completed.
- Run programme again to wash and rinse fabric.
- With fabric still in the machine, run the programme as normal with detergent or Synthrapol* to ensure removal of any excess dye.
- Remove fabric.
- Finally, run programme again to clean your machine.

Use 18 grms of Procion MX Dye Powder* to each kilo of dry fabric. Include more dye powder for stronger colours.

Preparing your fabric:
- For all the dyeing methods listed below – wash (scour) your fabric in your washing machine.
- Muslin and any loomstate fabric must be thoroughly washed to ensure a good depth of colour when dyeing.
- Add 1 tbls. of SYNTHRAPOL* (liquid detergent) to the washing machine to guarantee the removal of fabric dressing and greasy marks.

Wash your fabrics thoroughly. Ensure that fabric is still damp and unfolded, before commencing the dyeing process.

Paints for printing:
- Wear protective clothing, rubber gloves, goggles and a mask.
- Cover working surface
- Keep dyes out of reach of children

Assemble:
- Procion MX dye - 18 grms In chosen colours.
- Salt - 500 grms
- Soda Ash - 200 grms dissolved in 1 litre of hot, not boiling water
- Fabric (dry) - One Kilo
- Set washing machine to 60°C/140°F (warm) washing cycle

Hand dyed Muslin dress. Manipulated fabric and stitch.

MICROWAVE DYEING

(Using Procion MX Dyes)

- Pre-wash (scour) fabric as detailed above.
- Soda Ash Solution: soak your fabric for 15/20 mins in a solution of 100 grm of Soda Ash dissolved in 2 litres of water. Remove fabric and squeeze out liquid –keep for future use.
- Urea Solution: for each dye colour - dissolve 5grms (1 tsp.) of Urea in 100 mls water, at room temperature. Increase this amount for each dye colour .
- For one dye colour, dissolve 5grms (1 tsp.) of dye in Urea solution, less for paler colours.
- Place a large freezer or roasting plastic bag inside an old plastic bowl or box, pulling the edges of the bag over the edges of the bowl.
- Place damp fabric in the bag and spoon dyes evenly over fabric until thoroughly absorbed. Press lightly with gloved fingers, do not squeeze.
- Tie bag loosely to enable steam to be released and microwave on high for
- 2 mins. depending on wattage of your microwave. Check the fabric isn't drying out and microwave for a further 2 mins.
- Leave for two or three minutes to cool. Remove bowl and carefully release the steam. Thoroughly rinse and wash fabric.

Assemble:

- Procion MX Dyes*
- Soda Ash - 100 grms
- Urea - 5 grms (1tsp.) per dye colour
- Fabric – if using two colours, 50cms of fabric can be dyed with a skein or two of pre-soaked thread.
- 1tsp (old) - 5grms
- Large Freezer or Roasting bag.

Please be very careful, the liquid is very hot

HAND DYEING

(Using Procion MX Dyes)

- Pre-wash (scour) fabric as detailed above.
- Soda Ash Solution: soak your fabric for 15/20 mins in a solution of 25 grms of Soda Ash dissolved in 5 litress of water.
- Urea Solution: for each dye colour - dissolve 15grms (1 tblsp.) of Urea in 250mls water, at room temperature. Increase this amount for each colour dye you are using.
- For one colour dye, dissolve 4 tsp. of dye in Urea solution – less for paler colours. Stir thoroughly and replace lid on jar.

- Space Dyeing: Make up two or three colours of dye. Place damp, soda soaked fabric loosely in a shallow tray. Alternately spoon the dye colours evenly over the fabric. Press gently with gloved hands to ensure even coverage – do not squeeze. Place a plastic bag on top of fabric then wrap tray in a secured plastic bag to keep fabric moist and leave for at least two hours, preferably overnight. Rinse thoroughly as described for above.
- You can also lay fabric flat on plastic covered table and paint with colour to achieve graduated effects or spray dye with a spray bottle. Cover with plastic to exclude air and leave to cure for 2hrs or overnight.
- Thoroughly rinse as described in general dyeing instructions.
- Skeins of loosely tied threads – soaked in Soda Ash can also be added to tray.

Assemble:

- Soda Ash - 25grms dissolved in 5 litres of water.
- Urea - 15 grms (1tbls) dissolved in 250mls water
- Procion MX dyes* in chosen colours.
- Fabric: 18 grms dye to each kilo (2.2lbs) of dry fabric.
- Loosley tied skeins of thread (optional)
- Jars with lids
- Bowl or bucket
- 1 tbls and 1 tsp (old)
- 1 shallow tray approx.10cm deep

Why don't you try...
to block print onto Muslin

Most people would consider that printing on Muslin did not give very successful results, as a clear crisp image is not achievable. Nevertheless, it is the subtlety of the printed image that is the main attraction.

There are many approaches and techniques involved in printing images on fabric. This book just touches on block printing as a simple, economic but effective method of fabric surface decoration.

Monoprinting is another simple method of printing which is worth trying, because it too is, inexpensive and equipment is easily accessible

Study the suggestions listed on the following page and give them a go.

Hand printed Muslin embellished with stitch.

Block printing... springboard

Make your own printing blocks

Make your own printing blocks:
- Stick two pieces of mount board together and cut out a rectangle approx. 100cms x 120cms, though this is not critical. Use masking tape to make a loop on the back of the card to use as a handle.
- Stick double-sided tape all over the surface of the board.
- Try any of the following ideas to create designs on the card:
- Cut shapes from the mount board or from 'Funky Foam' – arrange in a design and stick onto the tape.
- Stick rubber washers onto board.
- Stick parcel string onto the board.
- Stick cocktail sticks onto the board
- Stick any suitable found objects onto board.
- Miracle Sponge*. A compressed sponge which can be cut into shapes. Wet the sponge and it expands. Can then be stuck onto card.
- WHEN BLOCK IS PREPARED – PAINT OVER THE SURFACE WITH WHITE ACRYLIC PAINT TO SEAL.
- Blocks can also be cut from a variety of materials such as Lino and softer alternatives – PZ Kut* and FlexiKut*.
- Press Print* Polystyrene sheets which you can press a design into with an old biro. A pizza base works as well.
- Heat & Form* – is a foam block which when heated with an iron can be impressed into with found objects to create pattern. Print with when cool, wash and use again. Protect iron and foam with baking parchment.

Prepare surfaces

Prepare surface:
It is essential to create a soft surface to lay or stretch your fabric onto when you print. For example:
a) A piece of blanket covered with a piece of old sheeting or calico.
b) Foam carpet underlay with plastic covering.
c) Half metre of table protector covering or Forming Felt*.
d) For small projects – foam table mats with plastic covering.

Preparing your fabric:
a) In most cases you need to thoroughly wash your fabric to remove any dressing. However, fabrics can be purchased that are readily prepared for dyeing and printing.
a) Iron your fabric to remove creases.
b) Ensure that your printing surface is smooth and then stretch your fabric onto your printing surface and either pin or secure with masking tape.

Paints for printing:
Suitable paints that you are likely to have at home or readily available:
a) Textile or Fabric Paints. These need to be heat fixed – not Silk Paints.
b) Acrylic paints – these do not need heat fixing. Because of the plastic molecules in acrylic paints, they can leave the fabric feeling stiff.
c) For metallic effects – the best medium to use is Bronze Powders. These need to be mixed with a fabric binder. One tsp. bronze powder to 1 tblsp. fabric binder. (Always use a mask when using these powders). Heat fix.
There is a wide variety of paints on the market, so make sure that you check the instructions on the label before purchase.

Print techniques

Print technique:
a) Lay fabric onto printing surface – stretch and tape or pin down.
b) Place a small amount of paint onto a printing palette.
c) Use a roller to evenly distribute the paint over the palette.
d) Roll paint evenly over print block
e) Impress the block onto the fabric surface.

Cleaning the blocks:

CLEAN BLOCKS AS SOON AS YOU ARE FINISHED WITH THEM.

Wooden and plastic blocks can be cleaned with an old toothbrush under the tap.
If you are using blocks you have made yourself, using 'mount board', just wipe with a damp cloth or wipes, such as baby wipes – do not put under the tap.

Commercial Stamps:
The 'stamping hobby' is at the height of its popularity – so there is no difficulty in finding retailers who sell stamps. Often a stamp will be offered free with a magazine.
Many good Art Shops and even some gift or interior design shops sell a wide variety of intricate Indian wooden printing blocks. Chosen carefully they are an excellent choice for printing with.

Dyed and printed Muslin embellished with stitch.

Boxes covered with Muslin – stitched and decorated with acrylics and Gesso.

Fibrefusion challenge

Monoprinting:

Monoprinting is a simple, quick method of creating a printed image. However, it's limitation is that you can only produce one clear and unrepeatable image. Don't let this put you off though, as with a minimum amount of tools, equipment and preparation, you can produce exciting, unique one off images, just ready for stitch.

Assemble:

- Apron and rubber gloves
- Cloths to keep area clean
- A print roller – firm
- A large brush or small household brush
- Acrylic or fabric paints
- A sheet of firm plastic i.e. laminator plastic sheets, OHP sheets etc.,
- Tools to make marks in paint i.e. old credit card (cut into one or two strips), old blunt knife and fork, lollipop sticks, old paint brush, roller.

Prepare:
- Cover your table with plastic
- Lay down a piece of old blanket or felt, bigger than your printing area
- Cover with an old piece of sheeting
- Cut out several pieces of Muslin and iron
- Stretch and pin one piece of Muslin to padded surface

- Apply paint onto your plastic sheet with either brush or roller – don't be too heavy with this or you will create heavy blotches of paint on the fabric surface. To avoid hard lines at the edge of your print, feather the edges of your paint with either brush of roller.
- Work quickly with your mark making implements to draw into the painted surface on the plastic to create a design.
- Carefully lift the plastic sheet and lay paint side down onto the stretched Muslin. Gently press and stroke the plastic all over to ensure an even print. Carefully remove by lifting from the corner of the sheet.
- Use cloth to wipe sheet and repeat the process if wished with another colour.
- As soon as you have finished printing, make sure you thoroughly wash the plastic sheet under the tap ready for further use.

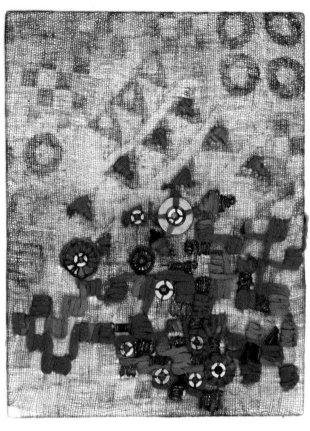

Muslin printed and stitched.

Muslin monoprinted and stitched.

2
Muslin and stitch

Stitching with loose weave fabrics often presents conflicting challenges to the embroiderer. On one hand you are able to wrap and draw the threads together both by hand and machine. On the other hand you cannot successfully work even and precise methods such as counted thread techniques. As embroiderers, you are challenged by the lightweight transparency and irregular weave of Muslin and Scrim – all the qualities that this book celebrates.

Muslin and light weight cotton Scrim are wonderful for working manipulated techniques and it is difficult not to get excited with the added visual effect created by torn and ragged edges. Strips of Muslin can be used to stitch with or woven as well as wrapping, coiling, knitting or couching. So many opportunities . . . so many decisions to make. Have a look at the following chart for suggested possibilities of how you can use Muslin with stitch. A myriad of stitch ideas are indicated in subsequent chapters:

Detail of strips of manipulated and stitched Muslin bag.

Bottom layer, painted Perspex. Top Layer, wired, stitched and distressed Muslin.

Muslin and stitch... springboard

	Hand	Machine
Muslin and print	• Print an image or images onto coloured Muslin and lightly embellish with hand stitch. • Print several simple, repeat images onto coloured Muslin, leaving a gap inbetween each image. Couch a thick thread in between the printed rows. • Print circles or shapes onto coloured Muslin in a grid-like fashion. Lay printed fabric down onto a coloured cotton background. Tack in place and embroider with running stitch around each circle. • Print circles or shapes as above – cut circles out leaving a 1cm border. Using same print block of circles, print a coloured cotton fabric. Using a contrasting coloured thread, work running stitch to apply the cut out Muslin circles onto everyother circle on the cotton fabric, leaving rough edges.	• Print an image or images onto coloured Muslin. Decorate lightly with free machine embroidery, just enough to compliment the printed image. • Print onto coloured Muslin. Cut printed image or images out and apply onto a dyed cotton. Free machine embroider lightly to compliment the printed image. • Try stitching with straight stitch, just in from the edge and leave the edges rough. • Working satin-stitch around the edges gives a neat finish, but don't make it too wide as it will dominate the printed image.
Muslin and strips	• Tear strips of Muslin between 1 and 2cms wide. Use these strips as a thread and stitch through both fabric and paper. Don't worry about the fraying edges, they add to the visual mix. • Twist the strips to make a cord and couch down by hand with a contrasting coloured thread. • Strips of Muslin can be woven, knitted, coiled or crocheted. • Use strips of Muslin to wrap either, wire, sticks, curtain rings, pieces of firm card or suitable found objects.	• A twisted strip of Muslin can be couched down with an open zig-zag using the machine. • Apply a 2cm wide strip of Muslin onto a background fabric by machine stitching down the centre – either with a straight stitch, satin stitch or a couched thread. Try applying three or four different coloured strips at once to enhance the rough edges.
Scrim and Muslin	• Muslin as a base (distressed) tacked to a watersoluble fabric. Cut Scrim into strips and stitch in rows onto Muslin. • Applied on top of Muslin – strips of Muslin woven together, leaving a deep fring showing. The two fabrics are stitched together. • Hand embroidery to embellish.	• Strips of Scrim can be couched down by machine onto Muslin. • Strips of Scrim can be woven to create a fabric, then free machine embroider into the centre. • Stitch beads onto the center.
Out of the ordinary materials to stitch into, or apply onto	• Paper or card • Hole punched metals • Lutradur* or Evolon* • Quality paper tablecloth • Wire Mesh • Moulding* or Forming Felt* • All kinds of plastic – punch holes if too thick. • Other openweave fabrics like Jute Scrim • Don't forget to consider recycled fabrics.	• Paper – all kinds but especially ethnic papers. Kozo paper is one of the stronger papers to machine into. • Lutradur* or Evolon* • Quality paper tablecloth (the type that resists moisture. It can be coloured with Dye-na-flow*. • Thin plastic bags etc., • Recycled fabrics

Fibrefusion challenge

The challenge

Sometimes lessons can be learned when you are set a challenge. The next few pages show work completed by the Fibrefusion group themselves – set as a challenge once the title of the next book was established.

The inspiration that everyone worked to was Seedheads. Everyone was given fabrics and threads set to a colour scheme – the main fabric being Muslin. They all received a piece of blue felt for the background, together with the instructions that the finished size should be a 15cm square. All the stitching was to be carried out by hand. (See pages 17, 18, 20 and 21).

Why don't you give this challenge a try?

Dyed and embellished Muslin decorated with eyelets and stitch.

- Two different coloured pieces of Muslin embroidered in lines with running stitch. Fabric slashed in between stitching.
- Muslin strips twisted and couched down. Echoed with hand stitch and Muslin tufts. Modelling Felt* embellished with straight stitches.

- Strips of coloured Muslin stitched with running stitch onto background layers of Muslin. Whole fabric embellished with Embellisher Machine.
- Edges frayed with Modelling Felt* used for detail.
- Straight stitches add emphasis.

- Modelling Felt* couched down for the stem.
- Long straight hand embroidery stitches to give detail.
- Tufts of Muslin stitched down with seeding stitches

- Modelling Felt* held down with couched thread.
- Shapes made with two layers of Muslin embellished with hand embroidery, straight stitch and fly stitch.
- Hand embroidery detail in background with straight stitches.

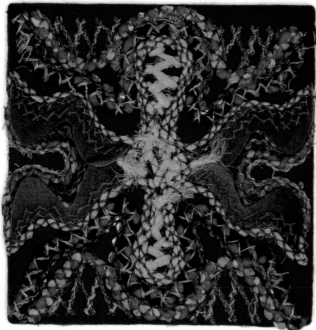

- Two different coloured rouleau made of Muslin were twisted together and couched down using herringbone stitch.
- Modelling felt* shapes were held down on one side with herringbone to achieve depth.

- Stems of modelling felt* couched down.
- Embroidery detail in straight stitch.
- Muslin bobbles anchored down with seeding stitches.

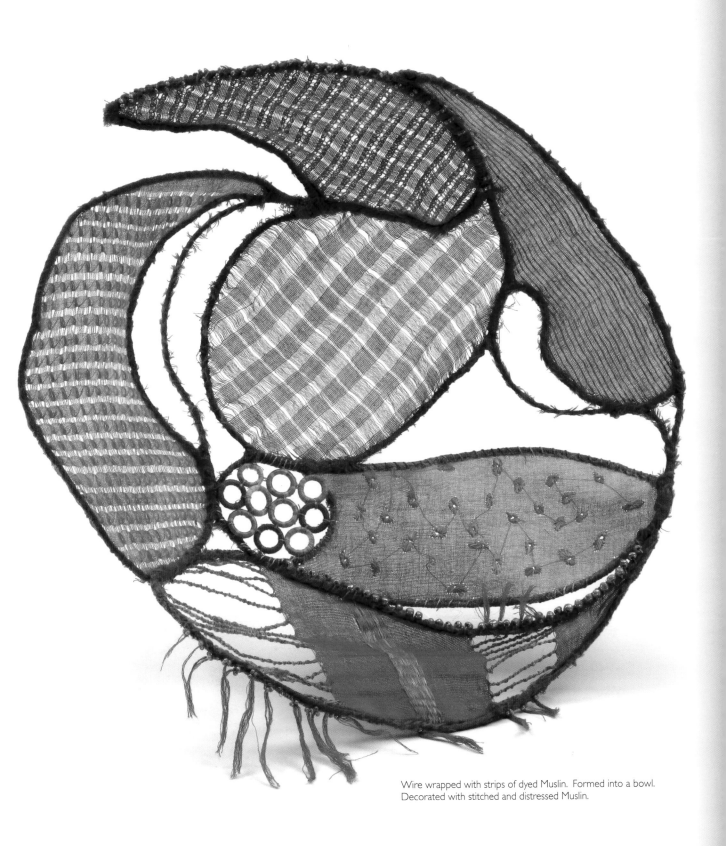

Wire wrapped with strips of dyed Muslin. Formed into a bowl.
Decorated with stitched and distressed Muslin.

- Background running stitches with strips of Muslin and thread worked into Muslin background.
- Rolled Muslin rouleau couched down with embroidery thread.
- Applied modelling felt* shape.
- Running stitch embroidery with french knots

- Main shapes – ruched Muslin with Muslin and hand embroidery detail.
- Long straight stitched and French knots.
- Rouleau twisted together and couched down

- Main shape two layers of Muslin padded in the centre. Embellished with running stitch and edged with herringbone stitch. Frayed strips of Muslin stitched down.
- Modelling Felt* shapes stitch down at tip. Cord couched down with French knots.

- Three layers of frayed strips of Muslin held down with couched thread.
- Wrapped centre stem.
- Modelling felt* circles wrapped with Muslin. Embroidered and beaded.

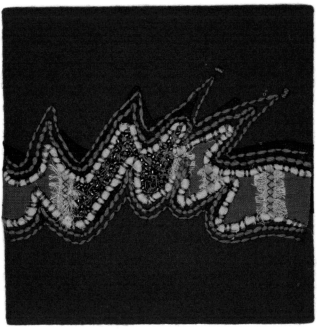

- Two layers of Muslin stitched down for background image.
- Rouleau couched down alongside couched threads.
- Modelling felt* couched down with cross stitch.
- Encrusted with beading and cross stitch.

- Square of Modelling felt* applied on top of frayed Muslin.
- Twisted Muslin strips with frayed edged couched down on top of another layer of Muslin.
- Embellished with beads and hand embroidery – french knots, herringbone, and running stitch.

Why don't you try...
to free machine embrioder on Scrim

Free machine a design onto Scrim:

- The design development process usually instigates choices for a colour scheme. Use your inspiration to colour your Scrim, either by one of the dyeing methods detailed at the start of the book, or by sponging or painting your fabric with Dye-na-Flow* diluted with 50% water.

- Choose your thread to either compliment or contrast with your dyed fabric - even using a little glitz if your design work suggests it.

- Place your design down on a flat surface. Stretch your dyed Scrim out over your design, securing the edges of the fabric with small pieces of masking tape. Lightly map out your design onto the Scrim using a soft pencil.

- Set your machine up for free machine embroidery. Frame up your Scrim – very firmly trying not to distort your design. Don't worry too much if the fabric ladders slightly, as this will happen when you start stitching.

- You are now ready to stitch your design using zig-zag on the widest setting.

- Having set your machine to zig-zag you will notice that your stitching will pull your threads together as you stitch, creating a pulled work effect.

Assemble
- Dyed Scrim, big enough to fit in your embroidery frame.
- Machine embroidery thread or threads.
- A design for your project.
- Soft lead pencil.
- Sewing machine set up for free machine embroidery.
- Basic sewing kit.

- Some of the lines you create can be machined over once or twice to create a bolder image.

- Shapes can be filled in with zig-zag, then alter your machine to straight stitch to tidy up and define your shapes.

- Machining on Scrim is a very satisfying technique to work with. Your finished work will be the stronger for the fundamental time spent on developing a design unique to you.

- With this technique you can stitch a complete design as described. It is also possible to just create a piece of textured fabric – cut it up and apply the textured pieces of fabric down onto another background forming a more three-dimensional piece of work.

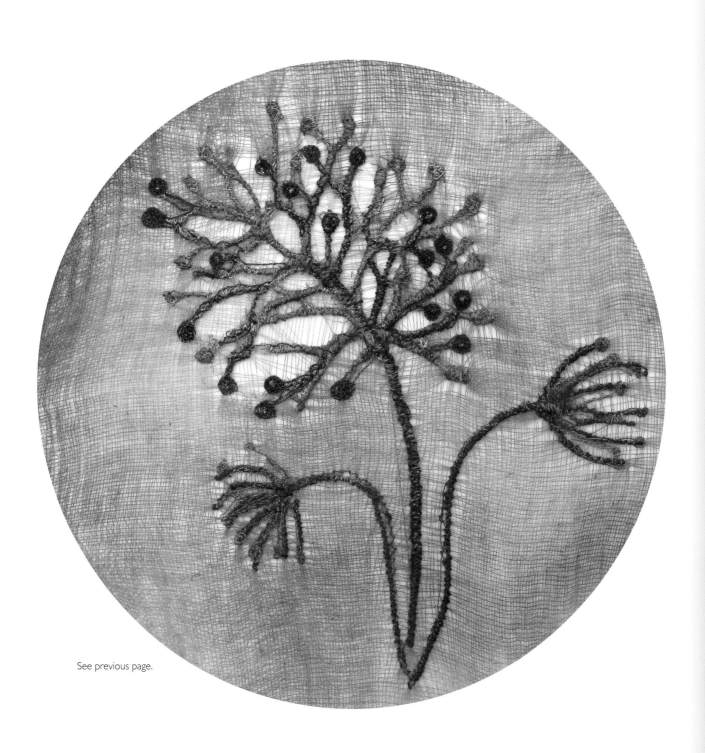

See previous page.

Fibrefusion challenge

Hold the front page

Embroiderer's like to experiment with a variety of materials – paper and newsprint being a popular choice. Trying to incorporate paper into your work can certainly bring challenges especially when hard paper edges, bold images and print need to become cohesive within the background. To this end Scrim works very successfully when overlaying a layer or layers to 'knock back' a conspicuous paper image bringing unity to a piece of work. Scrim is lightweight, soft and very loosley woven, so is perfect as a top layer to trap images and objects, to soften a strong colour or object or achieve a subtle, antique effect.

- Before cutting out – paint your newspaper headlines with a layer of Acrylic Wax* which has been tinted with any water based medium. Leave to dry, then cut out.

- Decide what you want to make and cut out your fabrics to size. Allow extra Muslin to chop up. Lay down the base fabric of coloured cotton. Place two or three layers of coloured Muslin on top.

- Chop up some of your spare Muslin pieces and scatter over the top of your fabric layers.

- Just put a little dab of glue onto the back of your laminated headlines and position them, paying attention to the composition of the design layout.

- Stretch the Scrim over the top, covering everything. Tack in place.

- Randomly free machine embroider the Scrim in place with a toning thread.

- Hand embroider running stitch around the headlines to highlight.

- This fabric is firm enough to be able to make a book cover, bag, or it could be the starting point to a larger piece of work.

Assemble
- Firm fabric such as coloured cotton or calico.
- Two or three layers of different coloured Muslin.
- Cut out some newspaper headlines.
- Acrylic wax* tinted with any water based medium.
- Coloured Scrim.
- Sewing Machine.
- Machine and hand embroidery threads.
- Glue stick or can of temporary glue.
- Basic sewing kit.

See previous page.

3
Muslin
layered & manipulated

Muslin is a soft, semi-transparent and diaphanous fabric. Given these qualities, it is the perfect material to create many forms of fabric manipulation. Consequently all loose weave fabrics become very versatile when placed in the hands of someone who is experienced in working with textiles. Manipulation offers further options when exploring the limitations and advantages of openweave fabrics to create texture, shape and form.

Embroiderers' use Scrim, Muslin and other open weave fabrics to pleat, tuck, ruche, fold, scrunch, gather, plait, twist and generally tease with the optimism that they will reveal a scrumptious textured and tactile surface.

Layering several sheets of different coloured Muslin together displays a soft thick fabric which is accessible for stitching techniques such as reverse applique. The edges of these layered fabrics also reveal a multitude of colours which can be exploited when working on your project. These effects can be exploited when creating jewellery, braids and lace, cushions, bags, book covers and even hangings. Muslin layers also produce wonderful results when worked with the embellisher, which we cover in Chapter 6.

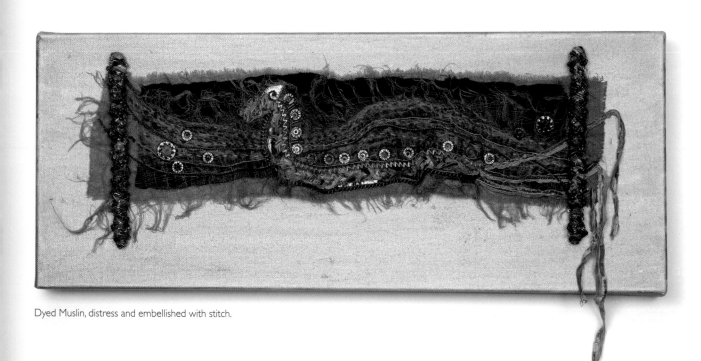

Dyed Muslin, distress and embellished with stitch.

Dyed Muslin dress –
manipulated and stitched

Fabric	Technique	Variations
Muslin Scrim Openweave Fabrics	Imagine that you are trying to replicate a design inspired by tree bark. Cut up small randomly shaped pieces of Muslin. Use your design to show where a raised surface is indicated and apply your Muslin shapes in a ruched style to build texture. Leave some flattened areas to show depth. Lightly stitch Muslin pieces down with toning thread, ready for further textural stitch by hand or machine.	• Paint your background. • Dye or colour your Muslin. • Colour your fabric and back-ground after you have applied your Muslin shapes. • Stitch lightly by hand or machine to add to the texture of the Muslin, not flatten it. • Ensure that your stitch connects all your shapes together to make a whole.
Muslin Some Openweave Fabrics	Cut or tear, 2 to 3cm strips of Muslin. Twist one or two strips together to make a cord. This cord can be couched down to add to the methods suggested above for creating a textured surface. It can also be couched down to edge and define a pattern. Strips of Muslin can be used to knit, crochet, wrap, weave or coil.	• Try using two or three, different colour strips of Muslin together. • The twisted cord can be couched down by hand or machine to fill shapes. • If couching onto another openweave fabric – try using a strip of Muslin as the working thread.
Muslin Some Scrims	Cut out circles of Muslin with approximate diameter of 4 to 5cms. With a doubled and knotted thread, stitch with small running stitches around the circle, just in from the outside edge. Gently pull the thread to tighten the circle – when half way – stuff with a scrap or scraps of Muslin, a different colour would be interesting. Pull thread tight and fasten off. Use these Muslin bobbles or Suffolk Puffs to apply when a textured surface is required.	• Stuff with different colours and types of fabric. • Stuff with coloured threads or fibres. • Stuff with sweet papers or foil. • When making a Suffolk Puff, display the smooth, rounded side uppermost. • You can also apply with the rough edges uppermost.
Muslin	Make a rouleau (tube) using Muslin (thick or thin). Stuff with coloured fabrics or thread. If making a thin rouleau, it can be couched onto a fabric surface as if it is a cord to create a linear design. A long thick stuffed rouleau can be couched down by hand so closely that there is no space left on the ground fabric. Use a firm fabric as the base to create a thick, soft fabric that is suitable for creating a bag or perhaps a cushion.	• A thin stuffed rouleau makes a good cord for a necklace. • Three or four rouleau can be plaited together to make a strong and firm handle for a bag. • Use a thin rouleau to tidy an edge of a book or bag. Stitch edges together, then couch down the rouleau by hand over stitched edge.

See page 40.

Why don't you try...
to free machine embrioder on Scrim

Most openweave fabrics work very well with various mixed media techniques because of the lightness and openweave of the fabrics. Scrim, which many of us were bought up to believe was only used for cleaning windows – has become an essential part of every embroiderers stash. If you want to achieve a distressed or antique look to a piece of work, then Scrim and a diverse selection of media is what you are looking for.

The distressed look

* Decide what you want to make and cut out your fabrics to the required sizes.

* Cover your table with plastic and lay your piece of sheeting or calico down. Spray lightly with water

* Spoon two separate amounts of 4 tblsps. of Gesso into your palette. Add approx. 1 tsp. of acrylic colour to each part of Gesso (different colours). Add 2 tblsp. of water and mix. Increase the amount for larger pieces of fabric. Increase the acrylic paint for more intense colours.

* Prepare your Scrim by cutting and tearing several holes in the surface. Make sure the holes cover the whole of the Scrim and generally distress. Spray lightly with water – make sure that it is all damp.

* Tear up pieces of newspaper picking out headlines and images into no bigger than 2 to 3 cms pieces.

* Randomly paint the surface of your fabric in the two colours of gesso mix.

* Press newspaper onto the Gesso whilst it is still wet. Paint over with Gesso mix.

* Quickly press your prepared Scrim into the gesso mix over your base fabric. Make sure that it sticks to the base fabric. Paint the rest of the gesso mix onto the distressed Scrim leaving no bare fabric showing. Leave fabric to dry.

* When your fabric is dry, rub fabric lightly over with Treasure Gold* or crayon/pastel in gold to pick up the high points of the textural fabric. You can equally use gold acrylic paint, just a little on a virtually dry brush catching the high points. Leave to dry.

* To finish the distressed look – free machine lightly with straight stitch in vertical scribbled lines. (See next image)

Assemble
* A piece of old sheeting or calico.
* Plant spray bottle filled with water.
* An old newspaper.
* A piece of Scrim – same size as sheeting or calico.
* Acrylic paint in chosen colours.
* Soft Acrylic Gesso*.
* Gold Acrylic Paint*, Treasure Gold* or gold crayon/pastel.
* Plastic to cover the table.
* Large brush and jar with water.
* Mixing palette.
* Sewing machine.
* Basic sewing kit.

See previous page:

See following page:

Fibrefusion challenge

Layered Muslin

When you layer sheets of Muslin together you can either make use of the thick, soft fabric that you have assembled or consider trapping threads, fibres or beads under the top layer. One of the most obvious and successful techniques is reverse applique or cutting back through the layers to reveal other colours. Consider trying some of the following challenges:

Muslin edging (Ragged Muslin Braid)

- Follow the list of materials and equipment needed in the 'Assemble box'.

- It is worth marking out your measurements on the top piece of Muslin – layering the colours together in order – tacking layers together, deciding the width of each piece of braid and then cut each length out if you are stitching the shorter length.

- Set your sewing machine up for free machine embroidery – straight stitch.

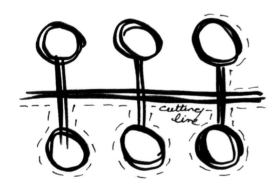

- Start stitching, just in from the edge of your Muslin layers and stitch the following pattern, making sure that you go over the initial stitched line two or three times as you go, filling the circles in quite densely.

- Continue the pattern until you have achieved your desired length.

- Using your embroidery scissors, cut the braid out, leaving a gap of approximately 3mm from the line of stitching. You don't have to be too careful with the cutting because you are going to 'rough' the edges up when you have finished.

- This edging or ragged braid can be applied onto the edge of

Assemble
- If you want to make a metre or more of this braid – use a metre of your main colour and half metre each of the two contrasting colours.
- For 56cms length, cut four pieces of Muslin 60cm long by 12.5cm wide – two pieces to go on top and bottom in one main colour. Two different contrasting colours (the measurements are approximate, as it depends on how much edging you need to make and how wide).
- Sewing machine set to free machine embroidery.
- Sewing thread to contrast with your main colour – could be one of your contrasting colours.
- Sharp pointed embroidery scissors.
- Basic sewing kit.

a cushion, or couched down in rows to make a fluffy cushion or bag. When you couch it down, it looks better if it is twisted as you stitch. See image on previous page.

- As a variation – cotton covered wire could be couched down the center spine so that the edging could be made into jewellery.

Construct a fabric

Wrap kebab sticks with strips of Muslin. Follow by wrapping hand embroidery threads lightly around the sticks. Cut wide strips of Muslin out and roll – making soft Muslin cords the same length as sticks. Create a grid by laying the kebab sticks down first and use cross stitch to anchor soft cords on top of wrapped kebab sticks (See example below).

Paper, Gesso and Scrim

Paper is stuck onto a Lutradur base. Work hand stitching with a thick thread onto the paper. The stitched paper is then painted with a coating of Gesso and the Scrim is pressed into the Gesso. Hand stitching and sequins are then worked into the Scrim. The whole piece is painted with coloured Gesso. See below:

Strips of dyed Muslin

Strips of dyed Muslin are knitted into squares. The knitted squares are heavily stitched using free machine embroidery straight stitch – in diagonal stripes. Eyelets are punched evenly around the edges. More eyelets are punched where the edges are joined. Pieces of coloured paper are then rolled to make tubes. Wire is threaded through the inside holes to join and create a decorative pattern: See below:

4
Muslin
three-dimensional

The definition of three-dimensional is having or appearing to have length, breadth and depth. Those who work with textiles have an affinity with working three-dimensionally, not only with items such as hats, bags, books, boxes, vessels but also with three dimensional works such as hangings and panels.

When using textiles to create 3-D items the obvious problem is how to make the work firm enough to hold its shape. We use wire and wire mesh, adhesives, heat guns, firm fabrics and card. Stuffing, knitting, weaving, wrapping, crochet, and coiling can, by manipulation and shaping, form a 3-D shape. Most of all, we must not forget, stitch which we use to manipulate and construct.

Moulding felt with Scrim – embellished – formed and stitched.

Muslin three dimensional... springboard

Materials	Technique	Variations
Scrim and Scrim strips	Cut strips of coloured Scrim then wrap and roll into small balls. Using another piece of coloured Scrim approx. 38 x 38cm, push a ball into the body of fabric – hold it tight and turn the fabric over. Your ball is now wrapped with the bigger piece of fabric. Using a needle and embroidery thread – fasten on and wrap thread around bottom of ball to enclose. Proceed in the same way with several balls, so it looks just like a bunch of grapes. (See next page)	• You could make the balls in two or three colours. • Your main piece of fabric can be bigger or smaller. • Use your bobbles to make a necklace or bracelet. • Use a string of bobbles as texture on another piece of work – or decoration on a bag.
Scrim and card	Use a piece of card to cut out a picture frame. Wrap with multicoloured strips of sheer fabric and threads. Distress a piece of dyed Scrim and overlay around the frame – securing at the back. Embellish with a variety of hand stitches. (See next page)	Use strips of machine embroidered Muslin to cover the frame. Cover with a piece of distressed Scrim that you have already stitched with free machine embroidery as seen in Chapter 2. Stitch beads on the surface.
Muslin and Strimmer cord	Use a length of white Muslin and oversew a length of Strimmer cord to it. It will naturally coil, so stitch as it lays. Paint fabric with dyes. When dry cut a thin strip of dyed Muslin and bind the cord, leaving the edges of Muslin rough. (See next page)	• Use pre coloured Muslin. • Embellish Muslin with free machine embroidery before attaching the Strimmer cord.
Muslin, wire tubing, two different wires, water soluble paper	• Lay Muslin onto water soluble paper and cut into thin strips. • Wrap the strips around a stick using fine wire. • Embroider buttonhole stitch randomly along stick. • Scrunch up Muslin and paper with wire. Wash away the soluble paper, remove stick and wind Muslin tube around wire tubing. • Thread thicker wire down centre of tube and twist all together. (See next page)	Stitch beads onto wire and Muslin tubing.

Wire wrapped with strips of Muslin and thread. Intertwined with tubular mesh and wrapped wire.

Dyed Muslin covered card. Wrapped and covered with threads and scrap fabric. Covered with distressed and stitched Muslin.

See previous page.

Why don't you try...
to create a vessel using Muslin and wire

Creating a three dimensional piece of work with fabrics as soft as Muslin and Scrim require some ingenuity. You have to work out how to achieve the required rigidity without compromising your vision of the finished piece of work. In this 'why don't you' section, we describe a method for making a three-dimensional vessel using wire and wire mesh as the means of firmly retaining its shape.

Create a wired vessel

- Decide how big you want your vessel to be so you can calculate how much fabric is needed. The vessel in our picture, is inspired by a Nigella Hispanica seed pod, so there are five separate shapes that are stitched together. When you have calculated the amount of fabric – double it and allow for shrinkage. This allows for the constructed fabric to be cut in half for the lining.

Assemble
- Approximately 1 meter of three different coloured Muslin.
- Large piece of fine Wiremesh*.
- Wire approx. 24 gauge.
- Sewing machine set for free machine embroidery.
- Embellisher machine.
- Machine embroidery threads.
- Hand embroidery threads.

- Layer your fabrics together and tack.

- Put your sandwich under the Embellisher machine and embellish thoroughly from both sides until the fabric is truly distressed and colours are penetrating through.

- Cut out a few small strips and squares from scraps of Muslin and apply decoratively to your main fabric, using free machine embroidery.

- Cut your piece of embellished fabric in half.

- On one half of your fabric, stitch rows of fine tucks using an overcast/over edge foot on your machine – this becomes the lining. If you don't have one of these feet, use one of the patterns.

- On the other half – using hand embroidery thread, oversew lines along the fabric, pulling the thread firmly to create little tucks (see example on next page).

- Cut out five pieces of Wiremesh* to fit the lower half of each of your shapes and tack in place on the lining.

- Wrap your wire with thin strips of Muslin – fasten off.

- Put your shapes together in pairs (a) the lining fabric with Wiremesh* (b) the outside fabric with hand embroidered tucks. Stitch all around the shape with sewing machine.

- Couch wrapped wire around the edge of each shape. Over sew each shape together by hand.

- From scraps of your lining and main fabric, calculate the size of the base and cut out. Oversew base in place by hand.

See previous page.

Fibrefusion challenge

Push the boundaries

As you stitch you accumulate knowledge and insight as to the materials you prefer to use and the techniques which you know work for you. It is therefore very easy to just sit in your comfort zone and not to keep pushing the boundaries and trying new ideas. Working with creating three-dimensional projects is one of those situations where the recognised method my be the easiest, but is it so aesthetically pleasing? Or even more importantly, does it fit the design criteria?

Coiling

Create a soft pot or vessel using the technique of coiling. Thread your needle with a strip of Muslin (working thread). Form a tight coil with the string (core thread), and using the Muslin strip wrap from back to front as per the diagram. Over one, over two, pulling with an even tension. As the coil gets bigger, work two small wraps and one long one, increasing proportionally the bigger the coil becomes.

If you want the sides to rise to become a pot, increase the tension and limit the amount of increasing stitches. Once you have made the pot to the required size you can embellish with hand embroidery as you wish. Painting either the inside or outside can also be effective.

Assemble
- Cut many thin strips of dyed Muslin for the working thread.
- Use either: strips of Muslin, thick cord or thick string and the core thread.
- A large eyed, darning or tapestry needle.
- Scissors.

Detail of coiled pot.

Make a bowl using abaca tissue and Muslin

Assemble
- Abaca or Lens Tissue*.
- Muslin or Scrim.
- An old pot or bowl.
- Cling film.
- Vaseline*.
- CMC Paste*.
  (wallpaper paste without anti-fungal additives)
- Jug of Water.
- Glue Brush.

- Tear the Abaca Tissue into 1 to 2cm pieces depending on size of bowl.

- Cut the Muslin into small pieces as above.

- Mix CMC paste according to instructions – make sure all lumps removed.

- Cover old bowl with cling film.

- Rub Vaseline all over cling film.

- Paint a film of CMC paste all over the inside of the bowl.

- Stick pieces of Muslin onto the glue base – pasting them in place as you go. Ensure there is enough glue on the Muslin to stick the next layer.

- Stick a layer of Abaca Tissue over the Muslin – pasting in place as you go. Build up eight layers, make the last layer Muslin.

- You can colour the bowl at this stage with fabric or acrylic paints, dyes or Dye-na-flow*. Heat set the Dye-na-flow* with hair dryer.

- Leave the bowl to dry thoroughly, inside and outside.

- When the bowl is dry you can hand or machine stitch inside.

- More layers of Abaca Tissue* and Muslin can then be added to the outside of the bowl to strengthen.

- Leave to dry again. At this stage you can apply pieces of stitched fabric onto the outside or print or paint to finish.

Make 3d items using modelling felt and Muslin

- Modelling Felt* is an acrylic wool mix felt specially treated to make it stiff. It can be moulded into shapes when sprayed lightly with water and left to dry. You can buy the Modelling Felt* in black, white, and a few other colours. This felt makes a really good substitute for Pelmet Vilene*. It is soft, thick, and you can machine into it. It also works well with the Embellisher. Hand stitching is very successful, as you can work on both sides of the felt by sliding the stitches into the surface.

- The most interesting effects are created when you colour the white felt. Spray with water on both sides of the felt and leave for 5 mins. so that the moisture has chance to penetrate the fibres.

- Make up a solution of Dye-na-flow* and water. At least 50% water – more for paler colours.

- Sponge or paint the colour all over the front and back of the felt. Leave to dry. Iron to heat-set the colour once it is dry.

- At this stage the Modelling Felt is open to any of the suggestions in the 'Ideas box'.

- One example to try is bonding Muslin onto coloured felt and create a bag as shown on next page.

- Bond or just stitch coloured Scrim onto the felt and try making bags, purses, boxes, book covers, vessels, books using the felt as pages as well. Try jewellery, hats or book wraps. (see examples on page 43)

Ideas for using Modelling Felt:
- Colour with dyes or Dye-na-flow*
- Print or paint on surface.
- Just use as a stiffener when making boxes or vessels.
- Bond onto one or both sides with Muslin or Scrim or indeed any fabric.
- Use for any fabric jewellery when a firm fabric is required.
- Stitch wire onto it to form shapes.
- As it is felt – you can easily cut out shapes and patterns on the edges.
- Use any of the layering techniques suggested in Chapter 3.

Coloured Moulding Felt* bonded with
Muslin. Hand stitched and embroidered.

Bag made with dyed and manipulated Muslin. Hand stitched to decorate.

Bag made of layers of dyed Muslin and recycled fabrics woven together and stitched.

Hat made from wire mesh, Muslin wrapped plastic tubing and Muslin flowers.

5
Muslin
embellish, patch & piece

When we talk about patching and piecing – patchwork is an obvious technique to think about. Patching together fabrics from old clothing and furnishings may be a traditional idea, but today we are once again looking at recycling fabrics. The wealth of different types of fabrics available to us today, motivates us with the desire to create something new and challenging from the old, worn out or 'out of fashion' clothes we have stashed away.

Muslin is not the first fabric we think of using when planning to piece and stitch fabrics together. The tendency is to think of crisp, strong, durable, and washable fabrics – mainly cotton. Don't let preconceived rules and traditions intimidate you. Push the boundaries to try and develop your own individual style, choosing unconventional fabrics, or dyeing, printing and embellishing your own fabric. Once you have identified and developed your design ideas or theme, allow your creative endeavors to bring a unique slant to your work. Develop your design concepts in a sketchbook using a variety of media, and then sample your ideas with fabric and stitch challenging yourself by using a variety of fabrics and techniques.

Unless you are piecing fabrics to make a warm quilt for your bed – have fun by trying to experiment with sheer fabrics, hand made felt, paper, metals, mixed media or using the Embellisher. Already you are starting to think out of the box, so let us start by looking at Muslin or Scrim or both for your next project.

Recycled and painted canvas. Torn strips of Muslin – hand stitched.

Scarf – embellished and stitched Muslin and wool fibres.

Muslin patch and piece... springboard

Materials	Technique	Variations
Scrim and Muslin	• Dye two batches of Muslin in contrasting colours. • Cut out four pieces of one colour Muslin and place on top of each other. Repeat with the other colour. Quantity of fabric is according to the project you are working on. • Embellish one layer of Muslin together and then repeat for the second layer (two layers in all). • Cut your two embellished fabrics into strips. • Wrap one colour around a metal frame or piece of card, leaving gaps in between. • Weave the second colour through wrapped strips and remove from frame or card. • Wind shirring elastic onto your bobbin under tension and randomly machine embroider to hold together and ruche fabric. (See next sample)	• Just strips of Muslin can be wrapped, not woven in both directions. Patterns can then be stitch to hold in place. • Strips of Muslin can be wrapped diagonally across the frame. Thick threads can also be added to the mix. Free machine embroidery on top.
Scrim and wire	• Use wire to form shapes, either circles, square, triangle, rectangles etc. • Using strips of Muslin or Scrim - wrap the wire to cover. • Use hand embroidery thread to lightly wrap the shape – sample on the next page shows squares. • Stitch all the squares together. (see sample on next page)	• Make wired shapes and wrap with threads and thin strips of Muslin. • Embroider in the center by hand or machine. • Stitch beads within the embroidery.
Muslin, wire and Scrim	• Form a circle with wire. • Wrap wire with strips of Muslin to cover. • Cut out a circle of Scrim, at least 2½ times the size of the circle. • Wrap the Scrim over the circle, pulling all the fabric into the center. Wrap the fabric with hand embroidery thread to create a tuft. • Work an open buttonhole stitch over the edges of the circle. • Stitch all the circles together. (see sample on next page)	• Use curtain rings instead of wire. • Wrap the center tuft with several ties of thread, securing but leaving the ends free. Before tying add a bead to either end of the threads.
Muslin and Scrim	• Cut out small squares of Muslin and Scrim. • On a firm background such as calico, stitch the squares down in pairs – one Muslin, one Scrim. • Cut more squares of Scrim to ruche and stitch in center of squares. (see sample on next page)	• Use coloured background fabric. • Couch a thread around inner edge of square. • Bead the center of ruched Scrim.

See previous page.

See previous page.

See previous page.

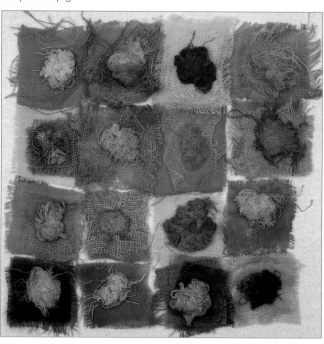

See previous page.

Fibrefusion challenge

Is it embellished or patched and pieced?

Because the Embellisher is becoming so much part of the stitchers equpment, it is sometimes difficult to distinguish between an embellished piece of work and a patched piece of work.

Basically, all our disciplines overlap which is one of the reasons we enjoy working with textiles so much. Therefore we may apply patches to a ground fabric, but we may also print onto them, embellish them and stitch into them with hand embroidery stitches – but are we are still patching?. Diversity is the spice of life and it means we stitchers will always have a passion for what we do.

Embellished or pieced

- Decide on what you want to make and calculate the amount of fabric needed.

- Cut four layers of different coloured Muslin and embellish heavily from both sides of the fabric. You need to distress the fabrics pushing colours through from both sides.

- Cut out small squares of a contrasting colour to lay on top of the fabric in a grid design.

- Embellish heavily once again.

- Hand embroider to decorate. (see image on next page)

Pieced, embellished and wired

- Cut strips of different coloured fabrics and stitch together by machine with the rough sides underneath.

- Using your now stripy fabric – cut again into strips, but this time horizontally.

- The cut strips are then stitched back together with the rough sides left uppermost.

- Lengths of hand embroidery thread are couched down by machine in between the strips.

- The fabric is then embellished, again in strips.

- Make little tucks in the fabric at intervals to encapsulate lengths of wire. Take care doing this to avoid broken needles.

Assemble
- Sewing Machine.
- Embellisher.
- Several colours of Muslin and Scrim.
- Hand embroidery thread.
- Wire.

See previous page – embellished or pieced.

See previous page – pieced, embellished and wired.

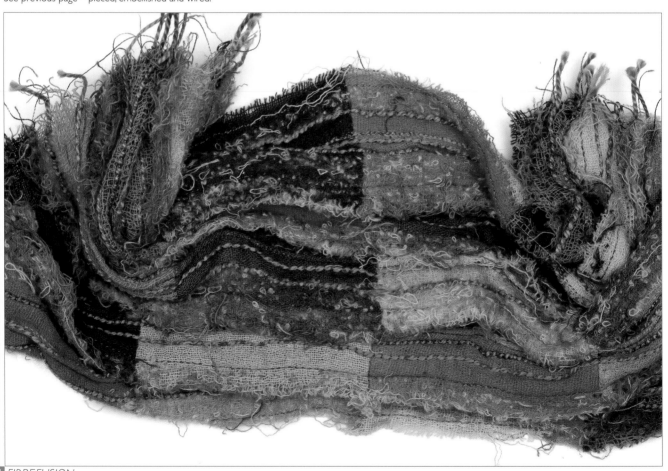

Muslin and the embellisher... springboard

Materials	Technique	Variations
Scrim and Muslin	• Make a fabric by embellishing two pieces of fabric together intensely from both sides trapping threads and fibres in between. • Cut into squares and embellish down in a grid pattern onto another piece of Scrim. • Lay a cord down along the grid lines and embellish. • Oversew the cord to decorate with hand embroidery. • Work rows of straight stitch in alternate squares. • See sample on next page.	• Cut any shapes other than squares and lay down in an asymmetrical pattern. • Twist a length of Muslin to make a cord and couch down randomly. • Work free machine embroidery to embellish.
Muslin strips	• Wrap a frame with lengths of hand embroidery thread. • Crochet lengths of Muslin in different colours. • Wrap them randomly around the frame, on top of the hand embroidery thread. Alternate the colours as you add them to the frame. • Embellish the fabric heavily on both sides. • Hand embroider chain stitch along the lengths of Muslin. • Cut off the frame. (see sample on next page)	• Wrap the crochet Muslin strips around the frame as a warp and a weft. • Wrap variegated wool over the top of the Muslin. • Embellish. • Work free machine embroidery in straight stich over the top of the fabric.
Muslin edging	• Layer two pieces of Muslin together in a main colour. • On the edge of the fabric, embellish a contrasting strip of colour from the back. • Embellish heavily, front and back. • Apply small squares of Muslin evenly along the edge to create a pattern. • Thread a needle with cut thin strips of Muslin and sew through the center of the small squares. • Tie in a knot. • See sample on next page.	• Lay two different colour strips of fabric on the back edge of your main fabric. • Embellish heavily. • Cut out small circles of Muslin and hand embroider down with a woven wheel stitch. • Stitch in the strips of Muslin as before, but bead the strips after they have been inserted.
Muslin tucked	• Lay a piece of Muslin down onto a piece of fabric. • Pinch about 2cm of fabric to create a tuck. • Embellish heavily along the tuck. • Keep embellishing tucks at right angles to each other all over the fabric. (See sample on next page)	• Embellish the Muslin heavily, on both sides over a bed of pieces of organza fabric. • Create tucks as described.

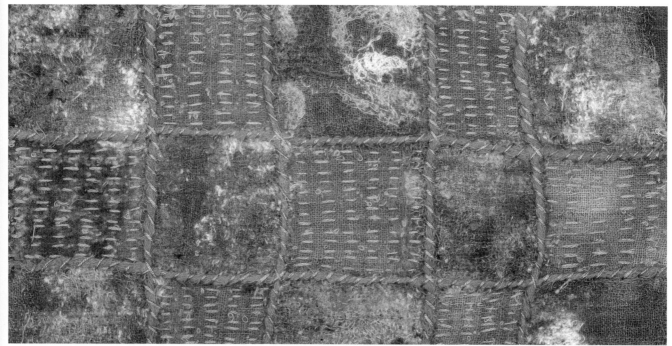

See previous page.

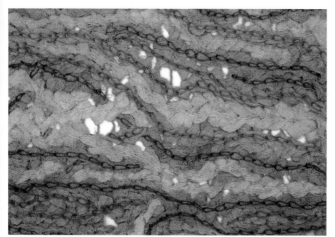

See previous page.

See previous page.

See previous page.

Fibrefusion challenge

All framed up

It isn't always necessary to go out and buy the latest new product on the market to achieve a stunning piece of work. We have threads, fibres and fabrics and a life time of experience.

The next and last challenges in Fibrefusion's book on Muslin is all about grids in one way or another. Why don't you challenge yourself to try out some of the suggested ideas.

Create an openweave fabric or net

- Dye your Muslin and Scrim in two toning colours.

- Layer two pieces of Muslin together.

- Cut out squares or rectangles of Muslin.

- Using watersoluble fabric, lightly tack the squares of Muslin into an open grid pattern leaving space all around the squares.

- Stitch an open mesh pattern (like a piece of net) into the watersoluble and over the squares of Muslin.

Assemble
- Sewing machine.
- Water soluble fabric.
- Muslin and Scrim.
- Hand embroidery threads.
- Basic sewing kit.

- Dissolve the watersoluble .

- Take your net and stitch it onto the two larger pieces of Muslin

- Scrunch up some Scrim and apply down into the centers of the Muslin squares.

- Embellish with hand embroidery. (See below)

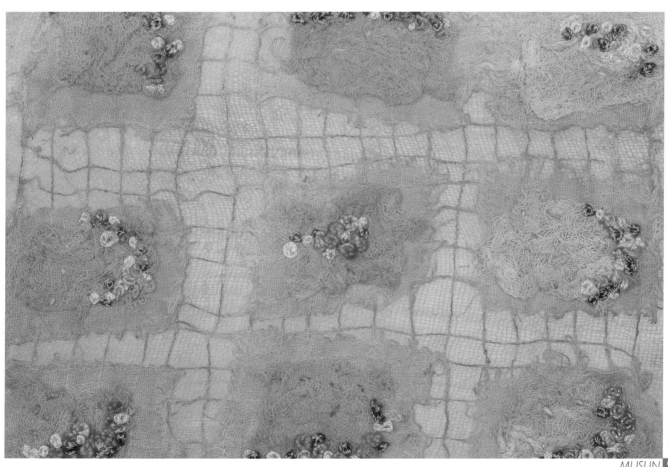

All wrapped up

- Wrap your frame firmly and under tension with shirring elastic – both a warp and a weft. Don't be too sparing with this or it won't work.

- Wrap the frame firmly with strips of thin Muslin in both directions.

- Wrap firmly two or three different coloured threads around the frame in both directions.

- Stitch lightly with free machine embroidery all over the fabric.

- Finally embellish the fabric heavily on both sides of the frame.

- Cut the fabric from the frame – it will ruche as you cut it away.

- To make sure that it is really scrunchy – gently roll and squeeze the fabric in your hands – it releases the tension in the shirring elastic. See below.

Assemble
- Sewing machine.
- An Embellisher.
- A square frame or card mount cut into a square.
- Very small amount of merino wool fibres.
- Muslin strips.
- Piece of organza 3cms bigger than the frame.
- Fine shirring elastic in a dark colour.
- Hand embroidery threads.
- Basic sewing kit.

Fibrefusion and Muslin

The girls (we say this rather flippantly), in Fibrefusion have had lots of fun compiling and writing this book. We hope you will have as much pleasure trying out some of the ideas and techniques as we have...

Stitched seedheads made from wire, Moulding felt, Muslin, Scrim and recycled fabrics.

Fibrefusion recommended suppliers

Art Van Go
1 Stevenage Road,
Knebworth,
Herts,
SG3 6AN

Full range of dyes, paints, printing equipment and accessories.
Wiremesh, Dye-na-flow, Acrylic Wax, Abaca/Lens Tissue, CMC Paste
Wide range of supplies for art and fabric art.
01438 814946
www.artvango.co.uk
art@artvango.co.uk

Dalston Mill Fabrics
69-73 Ridley Road,
Dalston, London,
E8 3NP

Good selection of coloured Muslin
Wide range of low cost quality fabrics
0207 2494129
www.dalstonmillfabrics.co.uk
info@dalstonmillfabrics.co.uk

Hindleys
24 Orgreave Place,
Dore House Business Park,
Sheffield,
S13 9LU

Modelling Felt, (white, black, red, yellow, green, blue)
Design and technology supplies
0114 269 1402
www.hindleys.com
sales@hindleys.com

Threads 'n' Things
124 Pheasant Rise,
Bar Hill,
Cambridge.
CB23 8SD

Wide range of materials for the textile artist,
Modelling Felt
01954 200731
www.threadsnthings.co.uk
lorna@threadsnthings.co.uk

Whaleys (Bradford) Ltd.
Harris Court,
Great Horton,
Bradford,
West Yorkshire,
BD7 4EQ

Extensive range of fabrics suitable for dyeing and printing
Full mail order service
01274 576718
www.whaleys-bradford.ltd.uk

21st Century Yarns
Unit 18,
Langston Priory,
Kingham,
Oxfordshire OX7 6UP

Specialises in unique hand-dyed yarns, threads, fabrics and
designs for all creative textile artists
07850 616537
www.21stcenturyyarns.com
info@21stcenturyyarns.com

* Strimmer cord and plastic tubing is available from garden centres
* Vaseline from any supermarket or chemist